How Willy got his Wheels

by

Deborah Turner & Diana Mohler

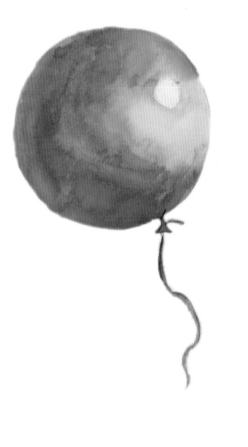

Illustrated by Rhonda McHugh

DORAL
PUBLISHING, INC.

Wilsonville, Oregon

Illustrations by Rhonda McHugh with thanks to Margaret Montag
Layout by Randy Conger of Universal Graphics
Willy's wheelchair manufactured by K-9 Carts, Big Sky Montana

Published by Doral Publishing, Inc. Wilsonville, OR 97070
http://www.doralpub.com
Printed in Hong Kong

Library of Congress Number: 98-70201
ISBN: 0-944875-54-8

Turner, Deborah.
    How Willy got his wheels / by Deborah Turner and Diana Mohler —
Wilsonville, OR : Doral Publishing, 1998.

    32 p. : col. ill.

        A tale of a little dog with a spinal injury who is adopted from the veterinary hospital and
fitted with all sorts of contraptions to help him get around. Finally a little wheelchair of his own
is devised and he becomes happy and independent. Appeal is to all children; teaches appreciation
for the handicapped.
        Age levels: 5-10 years old.

19980302155037.0   980217s1998   orualllj   000l1leng d

To all the homeless pets,
desperate to give love and be loved.
Let them enrich our lives.
Adopt a homeless pet.

Deborah Turner

For those of us with disabilities,
both seen and unseen.
Willy's example of living life
with exuberance and zest
is the best lesson he teaches.

For my family who give my life
its particular zest and exuberance.

Diana Mohler

Brrrrr! It was cold, cold, cold in little Willy's cage. The morning air was cold, the metal bars were cold, even his favorite fuzzy blankie seemed cold. Willy gave a big shiver. Brrrrrrr! He snuggled way down into his blanket so that only his face peeked out.

He pushed with his two good legs and tried to find a cozy spot to go back to his dream. It was the same dream he had every night: His back legs worked and he was running and playing with his family. Except he couldn't run and he didn't have a family. Willy lived at an animal hospital, because his back legs didn't work.

The blanket tickled Willie's nose so he yawned and sat up. He stretched his front legs, then pulled himself to the front of the cage.

Fred, the big bulldog in the cage next to him, saw that Willy was awake and wagged his stubby tail. It went thump bump, thump bump, thump bump against the wall of his cage. Willy liked Fred. When he barked, his **"WoooOOF, wooOOOOF!!"** was so loud it made Willy's whole cage shake. It made Willy feel safe. Fred had been there only two days and was leaving as soon as his broken leg was a little better.

"So when do you go home?" asked Fred.

Fred had a bad memory. He must have asked Willy this same question ten times already.

"I don't have a home," Willy said sadly.

"Gee, that's too bad. I play with my friend Tommy when he gets home from school. We go on long walks—well, we do when my leg works—and he throws the ball and I chase it. Sometimes I even chase sticks. I'm not picky, I'll chase anything."

"I wish I had a home," Willy said.

"I'm sure you will someday." Fred flopped down with a loud thump.

"If only my legs worked, I would run away and find a home where they would love me. Why, I'd be the best dog ever! No one would get past me, I would guard my family and keep them safe from harm. I'd be fearless." Willy sat up as straight as he could and imagined barking at a burglar. "Yep," he sighed, "fearless."

Willy imagined what it must be like to have a family, a real mom or dad who would love him. He'd sleep in a real bed, play with other animals, and chase sticks. Oh, wait, he couldn't chase sticks because his legs didn't work. That made him feel sad. But maybe he could find other things to do with his family.

Suddenly, he looked up and saw a pretty lady standing in front of his cage. She stood in the sunlight, which made her look like an angel. She just stood there and smiled.

Then he noticed that the doctor stood next to her. "Willy's back legs don't work," the doctor said kindly. "Poor little guy can only drag himself from place to place using his front legs. He's a good little doggy, but I'm afraid he'll never be able to walk like the other dogs. He can't even wag his tail. Are you sure you want to take him, Deborah?"

Willy looked up into her eyes. "Oh, please, please, please take me," he thought. "Pleeeaase?"

"Yes, I'm sure," she said.

YES! If he could have, he would have jumped up and done a back flip. He looked over at Fred, whose tail was thump-bumping against his cage as fast as it could.

Deborah reached into Willy's cage and gently lifted him out. "Oh, he's so small and thin, he hardly weighs any-thing," she said to the doctor. "Why, I bet just a little wind and he'd fly right off into the air."

She held Willy very gently. He felt very safe in her arms and snuggled closer. "The doctor tells me you need a home, would you like to live at my home?" Willy licked her hand to say 'yes.'

Deborah carried him out into the bright sunlight and placed him on a big, fluffy pillow in the front seat of the car. He sunk right down into the pillow. It was so soft and comfy, not at all like his cage. He tried to see out the windows, but couldn't. Willy was just too short and sunk too deep in the pillow. All he could see were the tops of the trees and the roofs of houses as they went by.

After what seemed to be hours, the car finally stopped. "We must be home," thought Willy. He wanted to see it! He gave one big push and he saw the top of a white house, then fell face first into the pillow. "Oof!"

Deborah laughed. "You sure are excited. You just can't wait to see your new house, can you?"

Willy smiled, then laughed. That must have looked pretty silly.

"Well, little Willy," Deborah said. "Let's go meet the rest of your new family."

She picked him up and carried him into the big white house.

"Sweet Pea!" she called when they were inside. "Come here and meet your new brother."

Willy heard a "click-click-click-click," as something trotted across the kitchen floor. A small blonde Chihuahua came around the corner and stopped. Sweet Pea tilted his head, first one way, then the other, then back again. Then he came right up and sniffed Willy.

His nose tickled.

Deborah carried him from room to room. Marshmallow—a large, fluffy, silver cat who was asleep on the footstool—barely glanced up from her catnap when Deborah introduced Willy. She flicked her tail, burrowed her face down under her paws, and fell back to sleep, which was her favorite hobby.

"Wow," he thought. "Now I have a brother dog *and* a sister cat to talk to and play with."

He could smell dinner cooking. It smelled wonderful. Deborah's home was bright and sunny, very different from the hospital he had just left. Everywhere he looked there was some-thing new to see.

Sweet Pea was fun to watch. He ran from one side of the room to the other and as soon as Deborah set Willy down he was there to tackle him. "Sweet Pea, behave," she said. He licked Willy on the cheek and then ran off in search of someone else to tackle.

Suddenly, there was a horrible racket.

Crash! Bang! **"Rreeoow!!"**
Marshmallow came shooting around the corner with Sweet Pea right behind her.
"Crazy dog!" Marshmallow meowed as she ran past. "Leave me alone!"

She jumped onto the couch, then up onto a shelf
where she sat down and frowned at Sweet Pea, who
laughed so hard he fell over onto his back. Then he wig-
gled around and around on the floor. He thought he was so
funny.
"Oh, you two." Deborah shook her head. "Don't mind them,
Willy. Sweet Pea just loves to chase Marshmallow."

Willy looked across the room and saw a big basket of toys. He pushed himself up and then tried to crawl over to it. It sure seemed a long way. "Oh, little Willy," Deborah said as she watched him struggle. "Here, let me help." She picked him up and put him next to the toys. There was a huge teddy bear. He tried and tried to move it, but couldn't.

"If only I could find some way to help you walk, then you could do things for yourself."

"It doesn't matter," he thought, "because this home is all I ever wanted. I'm as happy as I ever thought I could be." He found a little toy dog that was even smaller than he was and played with it instead.

The next morning, Deborah bought a big bunch of bright balloons. "Look, Willy," Deborah said. "Let's see if these big balloons can help you walk." He waited patiently while she tied them around his middle.

Marshmallow rolled her eyes. "This is silly. It will never work." She stretched out on her side, yawned, and tried not to act too interested in what was going on.

Deborah let go and Willy floated off the floor. "Oh, dear, this will never do," Deborah said. "You can't walk if you're not on the ground." Sweet Pea laughed and fell over.

"It's okay. I'm having fun. Look, I'm flying!" It felt wonderful to float around the room.

Marshmallow lifted her head, snorted, and shook her head. "Silly." She sighed and rolled over.

Deborah got him down and undid the balloons. She looked sad that her idea hadn't worked. She scratched her head and thought. "Hmmmm . . ." she said "what can we try next?" Suddenly, she snapped her fingers and ran out the door.

Sweet Pea, Willy, and Marshmallow all looked at each other. "Now where is she going?" they asked. Sweet Pea jumped up on the couch and looked out the window.

"She's talking to the boy next door," he said.

"What are they saying?" Willy asked. He wished he could climb up on the couch. Then he could see for himself.

"I don't know, I can't hear. But he's nodding his head . . . Oh, wait, now he's giving her something," Sweet Pea said. "Look out! Here she comes." He quickly jumped off the couch, ran over to the door, skidded to a stop, and sat down in front of it.

The door flew open and Deborah came in, all out of breath. She had run back home and was very excited. In her hands, she held a strange board that had wheels attached to it. What was it?

"Look, Willy! Look what I have. Let's try this skateboard!" she said.

A skateboard? Willy had never seen a skateboard before. What were they used for? How did they work? She put him on the skateboard with his front legs touching the floor. He felt it slowly slide out from under him. "Whoa," he thought. "I don't know about this." He felt a little scared, but waited patiently to see what would happen next.

"Silly," Marshmallow said. She jumped down off her shelf and walked into the kitchen, flicking her tail. "It will never work."

Using a shoestring, Deborah tied Willy in place. "This should help you walk."

Deborah let go of the board and Willy started to walk. The board was a little heavy. So she helped him get started by giving him a little push.

That helped all right, but then the board started
going faster and faster and faster and Willy's legs
could hardly keep up.

He couldn't stop! The board rolled right across
the living room and out into the kitchen where the
slippery floor made him go even faster!

"Yikes!" he yelled as he shot across the
floor. He tried to steer with his legs but
nothing happened.

"Look out!" he yelled to Marshmallow who was quietly taking a drink. Marshmallow looked up and saw a crazy dog on a big skate-board rolling right at her!
"**Meeeooooww!**"

Marshmallow turned and ran with Willy right behind her.
"Look out, look out!" he yelled.
"I am I am!" she yelled.

Too late! Willy smashed into the back of her and Marshmallow landed right on top of him. Willy tried even harder to steer. He got them turned around but they still couldn't stop!

"Look out!" Willy and Marshmallow both yelled as they zoomed into the living room.

Sweet Pea and Deborah jumped out of the way.

Willy and Marshmallow flew past and crashed into Willy's mattress.

"**OOOoof!**" he said. "No brakes."

"Crazy dog," said Marshmallow. She shook her head, patted down her fur, then stomped out of the room.

Sweet Pea was holding his sides he was laughing so hard. "You should have seen yourself," he finally said. "Your eyes were as big as soccer balls."

Willy and Deborah laughed, too. "That was quite a ride," she said. "Luckily, no one got hurt." Deborah gently untied the shoestring and picked him up. "Well, the skateboard wasn't the answer, but it's a start. And . . . it gives me an idea."

Over the next few weeks, Deborah carried him everywhere and he thought that was fun, too, but he still wished he could do things on his own. Even though the skateboard idea hadn't worked, it had been fun for a little while to be able to move like that.

Deborah seemed to be waiting for something, but Willy had no idea what.

Then one day, a big truck rumbled up to their house and then stopped with a "squeeeak" and a "hiiiissss." A tall man climbed down from the truck and said, "I have a delivery for little Willy."

He carried a big box with a huge red bow right into the living room and set it down.

Marshmallow sat up straight and Sweet Pea jumped up and down. "What ever could it be?" Willy wondered.

Deborah smiled and said, "I have a surprise for you." He watched as she slowly unwrapped the package. She pulled out a strange, shiny metal object with wheels.

"Oh no, not another skateboard!" Willy groaned.

FOR WILLY

But this was different. It had soft red straps and was much smaller than the skateboard. He'd never seen anything like it. What could it be?

"Here, Willy," Deborah said, "this is for you." She picked him up and put his rear legs through the padded straps of his new wheelchair. Then she buckled him in.

Willy was so excited, he couldn't wait to try it! His little front legs were already moving before Deborah could put him down. As soon as she did, he took off across the floor just as fast as he could. He raced into the kitchen, spun around, and zoomed back into the living room.

"Wheeee!" he cried. "Look at me! Look at me go!"

Marshmallow, remembering the last time Willy had wheels, jumped back on to the couch, but not up to her shelf. She didn't know what to make of all this.

"I can walk, I can run, why, I can fly!" Willy ran off to the kitchen, shouting,"I'm free, I'm free!" Then he ran back in to the living room, stopped, and spun around.

"Look, Sweet Pea, I can chase you now." And he did! He chased Sweet Pea around the living room until Sweet Pea jumped up on the couch next to Marshmallow. No one had ever chased <u>him</u> before. "I don't know if this is such a good idea," he complained to Marshmallow.

Willy ran around and around Deborah. He was so happy!

"Wow! I never knew it could be like this!" he said.

Marshmallow rolled her eyes. "I guess now we'll have to call him 'Wheely Willy.'"

Deborah opened the door and Willy raced outside into the warm sunshine. Marshmallow and Sweet Pea followed. Why, the yard looked so huge and inviting to Willy. And now he could go anywhere in it he wanted! The flowers were blooming and smelled wonderful. He ran to sniff the roses, then chased a butterfly that had been napping on one.

He stared at the rose and thought for a moment. He suddenly felt very differ-ent inside. He thought back to the hospital and his little cage, how the doctor had always had to take care of him. Even in his new home, Deborah had to carry him. Everybody needs to be able to do what they want to do, and it felt so good to do things on his own now. And that made him feel big and important.

He looked at Deborah's house, his home, and then he looked around outside. The world was huge and inviting. "I'm ready for you world. I have everything I need to face whatever comes my way. I have my family to love me, my wheels, and I'm ready to go!"

Marshmallow went back inside and watched them chase each other from the window. "Things sure are going to be different around here, now that he has his wheels. Who knows where those wheels are going to take him?"

She just shook her head. "And I just *know* that crazy little dog is going to be chasing me all around the house in no time."

The End

Willy currently lives in Long Beach, California with Deborah Turner and close to his friend, Diana Mohler.

Nobody knows how Willy's legs were injured, but he really does get around in a little wheelchair that was made just for him. He loves children and loves to make people smile wherever he goes. He's even been in a marathon.

But <u>that</u> is another story . . .